READING POWER

Doug Flutie
International Football Star
Rob Kirkpatrick

The Rosen Publishing Group's
PowerKids Press ™
New York

For Suzi and the P.I. Posse.

Published in 2000 by The Rosen Publishing Group, Inc.
29 East 21st Street, New York, NY 10010

First Edition

Book design: Michael de Guzman

Photo Credits: pp. 5, 7 © Ezra O. Shaw/Allsport; p. 9 © Eliot Schechter/Allsport; pp. 11, 13, 22 © Rick Stewart/Allsport; p. 15 © Damian Strohmeyer/Allsport; p. 17 © Caryn Levy/Allsport; p. 19 © Zoran Milich/Allsport; p. 21 © Reuters/Dave Buston/Archive Photos.

Text Consultant: Linda J. Kirkpatrick, Reading Specialist/Reading Recovery Teacher

Kirkpatrick, Rob.
  Doug Flutie : international football star / by Rob Kirkpatrick.
   p. cm. — (Reading power)
  Includes index.
  SUMMARY: Introduces the quaterback for the Buffalo Bills, Doug Flutie, who has also played in the Canadian Football League.
   ISBN 0-8239-5537-0
   1. Flutie, Doug Juvenile literature. 2. Football players—United States Biography Juvenile literature. 3. Canadian Football League Juvenile literature. 4. Buffalo Bills (Football team) Juvenile literature. [1. Flutie, Doug. 2. Football players.] I. Title. II. Series.
   GV939.F59 K57 1999
   796.332'092—dc21
   [B]   99-16003
                   CIP

Manufactured in the United States of America

Contents

Doug Flutie plays football.
He is a quarterback.

5

Doug plays for the Buffalo Bills. He is number 7 on the Bills.

Doug is good at throwing the ball. When he throws the ball, it is called a pass. Doug loves to pass the ball.

9

Doug can run with the ball.
He is very fast.

11

Fans love to see Doug play. He gets a lot of points for the Bills.

13

Doug has played for a lot of teams. He played for the Patriots.

Doug played for the
Chicago Bears.

Doug has passed for a lot of teams. He even played in Canada. He liked throwing passes in Canada.

Doug won the Grey Cup
in Canada.

Doug is happy to play in America now. He loves to play football everywhere. He loves it when his team wins, too.

Here are more books to read about Doug Flutie and football:

Doug Flutie (A New True Book)
by Ray Broekel
Children's Press (1995)

Football Stars (All Aboard Reading)
by Jim Campbell, illustrated by
Sydelle A. Kramer
Grosset & Dunlap (1997)

To learn more about football, check out this Web site:

http://www.nfl.com

Glossary

fans (FANZ) People who like to see games.

Grey Cup (GRAY KUHP) A prize for the best football team
   in Canada.

pass (PAS) When a quarterback throws the ball to a player.

quarterback (KWAR-ter-bak) The player who throws the ball.

Index

Word Count: 136

Note to Librarians, Teachers, and Parents

If reading is a challenge, Reading Power is a solution! Reading Power is perfect for readers who want high-interest subject matter at an accessible reading level. These fact-filled, photo-illustrated books are designed for readers who want straightforward vocabulary, engaging topics, and a manageable reading experience. With clear picture/text correspondence, leveled Reading Power books put the reader in charge. Now readers have the power to get the information they want and the skills they need in a user-friendly format.